Europe

Teaching Tips

Gold Level 9
This book focuses on developing reading independence, fluency, and comprehension.

Before Reading
- Ask readers what they think the book will be about based on the title. Have them support their answer.

Read the Book
- Encourage readers to read silently on their own.
- As readers encounter unfamiliar words, ask them to look for context clues to see if they can figure out what the words mean. Encourage them to locate boldfaced words in the glossary and ask questions to clarify the meaning of new vocabulary.
- Allow readers time to absorb the text and think about each chapter.
- Ask readers to write down any questions they have about the book's content.

After Reading
- Ask readers to summarize the book.
- Encourage them to point out anything they did not understand and ask questions.
- Ask readers to review the questions on page 23. Have them go back through the book to find answers. Have them write their answers on a separate sheet of paper.

© 2024 Booklife Publishing
This edition is published by arrangement with Booklife Publishing.

North American adaptations © 2024 Jump!
5357 Penn Avenue South
Minneapolis, MN 55419
www.jumplibrary.com

Decodables by Jump! are published by Jump! Library.
All rights reserved. No part of this book may be reproduced in any form without written permission from the publisher.

Library of Congress Cataloging-in-Publication Data is available at www.loc.gov or upon request from the publisher.

ISBN: 979-8-88996-918-1 (hardcover)
ISBN: 979-8-88996-919-8 (paperback)
ISBN: 979-8-88996-920-4 (ebook)

Photo Credits
Images are courtesy of Shutterstock.com. With thanks to Getty Images, Thinkstock Photo and iStockphoto. Cover – NaMong Productions. p4–5 – Pyty, ixpert. p6–7 – Pyty, xbrchx. p8–9 – Sergey Novikov, BearFotos. p10–11 – Creative Travel Projects, ixpert, thegrimfandango. p12–13 – Pav-Pro Photography Ltd, Albert Beukhof. p14–15 – Serg64, svetkor, Olena Znak. p16–17 – Joerg Beige, Yury Dmitrienko, Alexander Raths. p18–19 – Stuart Monk, Anna Moskvina, Daniel_Kay. p20–21 – Kite_rin, jocic.

Table of Contents

Page 4   What Is a Continent?

Page 6   Europe

Page 8   Languages

Page 10 Weather

Page 12 Animals

Page 14 Plants and Trees

Page 16 Food

Page 18 United Kingdom

Page 20 Greece

Page 22 Index

Page 23 Questions

Page 24 Glossary

What Is a Continent?

A continent is a very large area of land. Our planet is split into seven continents. Most of these continents have many countries within them.

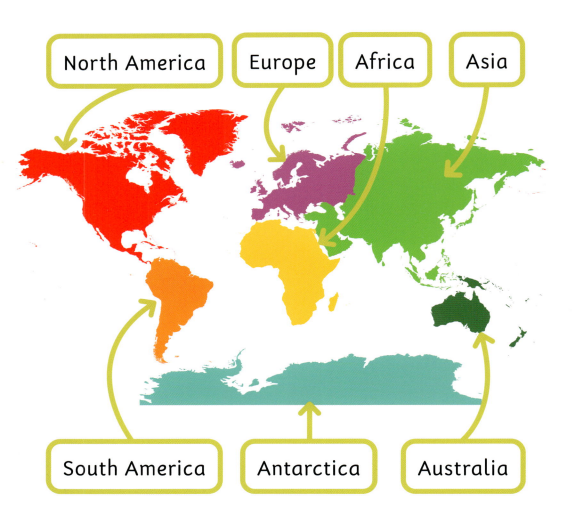

Each continent is very different from the others. They each have different weather and landscapes. People in different areas may have different ways of life.

Europe

Europe is one of the seven continents. It is north of Africa and west of Asia. Europe is the second smallest continent, yet there are 50 countries in Europe, including France, Romania, and western Russia.

Europe might be small, but more than 740 million people live there! From busy cities and sunny beaches to snowy mountains, Europe has lots of different **climates** and landscapes. Europe is also full of amazing buildings and history.

Languages

Around 200 different languages are spoken in Europe. Some of these languages, such as English, are spoken by many people across the continent. Other languages, such as Flemish, are only spoken by people in a small part of one country.

People who live in Europe are known as Europeans. Many Europeans are bilingual. This means they can speak and understand two languages. Many countries have an official language, which is the language most people speak.

Weather

The equator is an invisible line that runs along Earth's middle. Places close to the equator are warmer than places farther away. Europe is north of the equator.

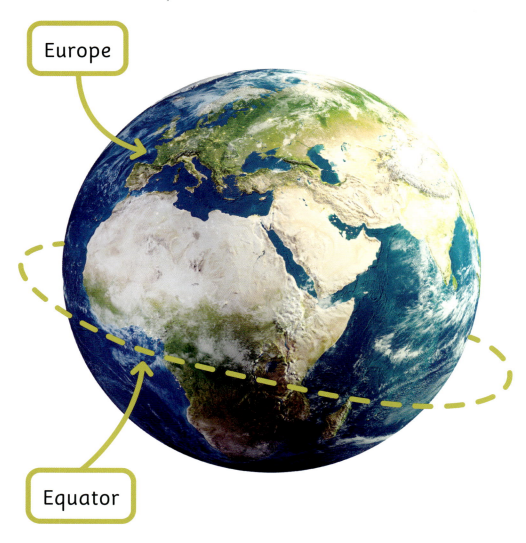

Europe

Equator

Europe has different types of weather. It has four seasons called winter, spring, summer, and fall. It gets colder in winter and warmer in summer. Countries in northern Europe tend to be colder than southern countries.

Snowy Finland

Sunny Italy

Animals

Many different animal **species** live in Europe. Many of them have **adapted** to live there. Reindeer are found in the cold northern countries of Norway, Sweden, Finland, Greenland, and Russia. Their thick fur coats keep them warm.

Reindeer

Many animals have clever ways of handling the changing seasons. During winter, it can be much harder for animals to find food. Animals such as mice, squirrels, and hedgehogs **hibernate** during these months to save energy.

Squirrel

Plants and Trees

Just like animals, many plants can only live in certain areas. Pine trees have adapted to grow in cold parts of Europe. Their trunks are covered in thick bark that protects them from the harsh weather.

Pine trees

Many flowers bloom in spring and summer when it is warmer. During spring, tulips bloom in the Netherlands. In France, lavender and sunflowers bloom during summer. Besides looking pretty, these flowers can also be used in cooking.

Food

There are millions of people in Europe, and everyone has to eat! Lots of European countries are famous for different types of food. Let's look at some tasty food from Europe! Bratwurst is a type of sausage from Germany.

Belgium is known for waffles. Belgian waffles are often served with fruit and chocolate. Bukta is a sweet bread filled with jam that comes from Hungary. For many countries, food is an important part of their **culture**.

Belgian waffles

Bukta

United Kingdom

The United Kingdom is made up of four countries. England, Scotland, and Wales are on one island, and Northern Ireland is on another. The biggest city in the United Kingdom is London. London is also England's capital city.

London

There are lots of different landscapes in the United Kingdom. Because it is an island, it has lots of beaches. It also has mountains and forests that are full of **wildlife**.

Greece

Greece is in southeast Europe. Greece is one of the closest European countries to the equator. Summers there can get very hot. Lots of people visit Greece to enjoy the warm weather.

Many people in Greece live in cities. Some people also live in villages and towns in the countryside. The tallest mountain in Greece is Mount Olympus. This mountain is very important in Greek **mythology**.

Mount Olympus

Index

equator 10, 20
Norway 12
squirrels 13
waffles 17
winter 11, 13

How to Use an Index

An index helps us find information in a book. Each word has a set of page numbers. These page numbers are where you can find information about that word.

Page numbers

Example: balloons 5, <u>8–10</u>, 19

Important word

This means page 8, page 10, and all the pages in between. Here, it means pages 8, 9, and 10.

Questions

1. How many continents are there?

2. Why do squirrels hibernate in winter?

3. What is the name of the tallest mountain in Greece?

4. Using the Table of Contents, can you find which pages have information about European food?

5. Using the Index, can you find a page in the book about the equator?

6. Using the Glossary, can you define what climates are?

Glossary

adapted:
Changed to suit different conditions.

climates:
Weather that is typical of certain areas.

culture:
The beliefs and practices of a specific group of people.

hibernate:
To sleep for the whole winter.

mythology:
A series of myths or stories from a culture.

species:
One of the groups into which similar animals and plants are divided.

wildlife:
Wild creatures such as birds, mammals, and fish.